NEW Chatterbox

Starter

Activity Book

Charlotte Covill

OXFORD
UNIVERSITY PRESS

● **Colour.**

● **Match and draw.**

   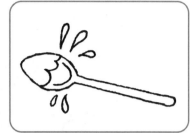

● **Read and colour.**

Look

Listen

Stand up

Sit down

Open your book

Close your book

● **Count and match.**

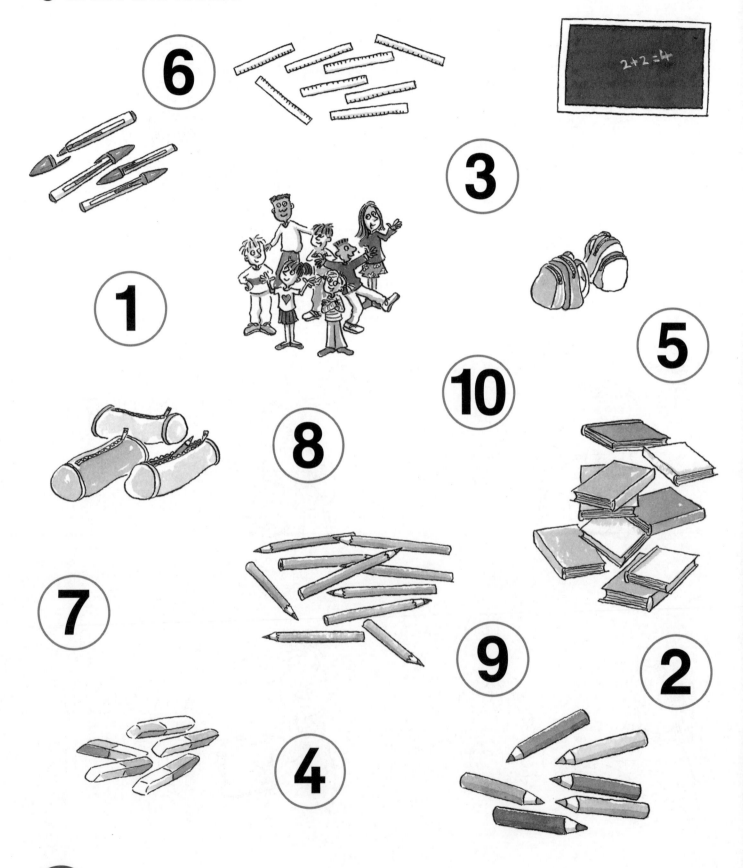

THE DONUT MAN

● **Match and draw.**

Pluto   Donut Joe

● **Circle 5 differences.**

● **Find and circle.**

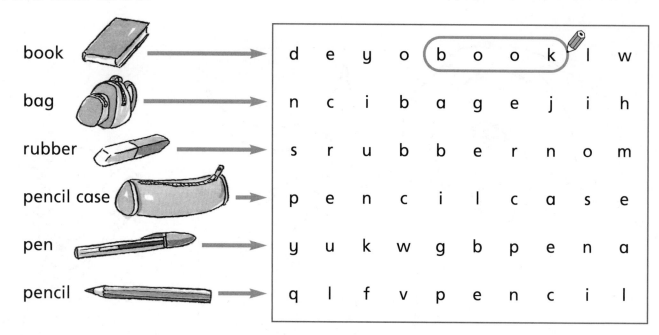

book

bag

rubber

pencil case

pen

pencil

d	e	y	o	b	o	o	k	l	w
n	c	i	b	a	g	e	j	i	h
s	r	u	b	b	e	r	n	o	m
p	e	n	c	i	l	c	a	s	e
y	u	k	w	g	b	p	e	n	a
q	l	f	v	p	e	n	c	i	l

● **Draw and say.**

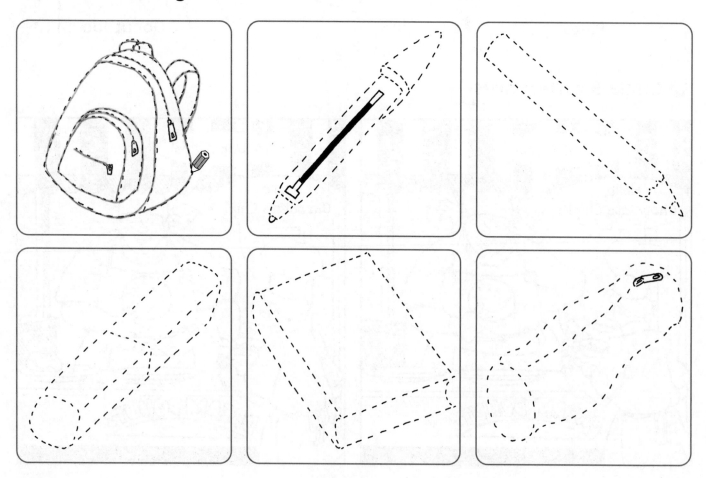

● **Look and number.**

my mum ☐4 my dad ☐ my brother ☐ my sister ☐

● **Write.**

my mum

my dad

my brother

my sister

LET'S GO!

● **Match and draw.**

● **Find and match.**

my mum | my dad | my brother | my sister

Who's this?

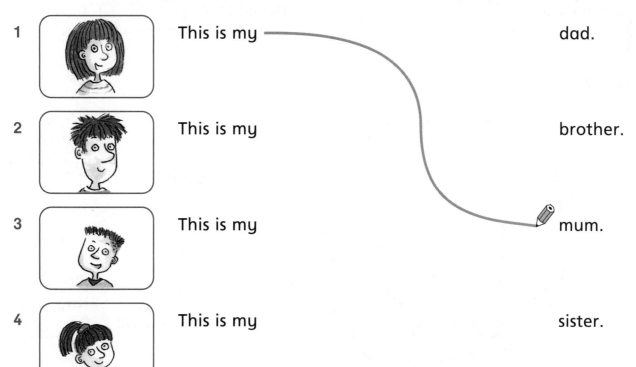

1 This is my   dad.

2 This is my   brother.

3 This is my   mum.

4 This is my   sister.

Project time!

● Look and ✔ or ✗.

bag		☐
pencil		☐
rubber		☐
pen		☐
book		☐
pencil case		☐

bag		☐
pencil		☐
rubber		☐
pen		☐
book		☐
pencil case		☐

● Draw and ✔ or ✗.

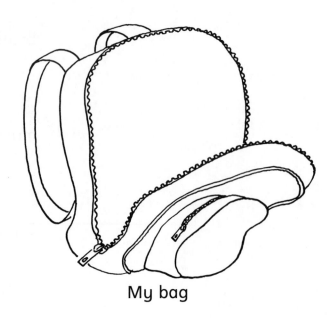

My bag

bag		☐
pencil		☐
rubber		☐
pen		☐
book		☐
pencil case		☐

● **Colour.**

● **Read and colour.**

red

yellow

green

blue

black

white

WHO'S THIS?

● **Write the number.**

● **Colour.**

● **Find, count and write.**

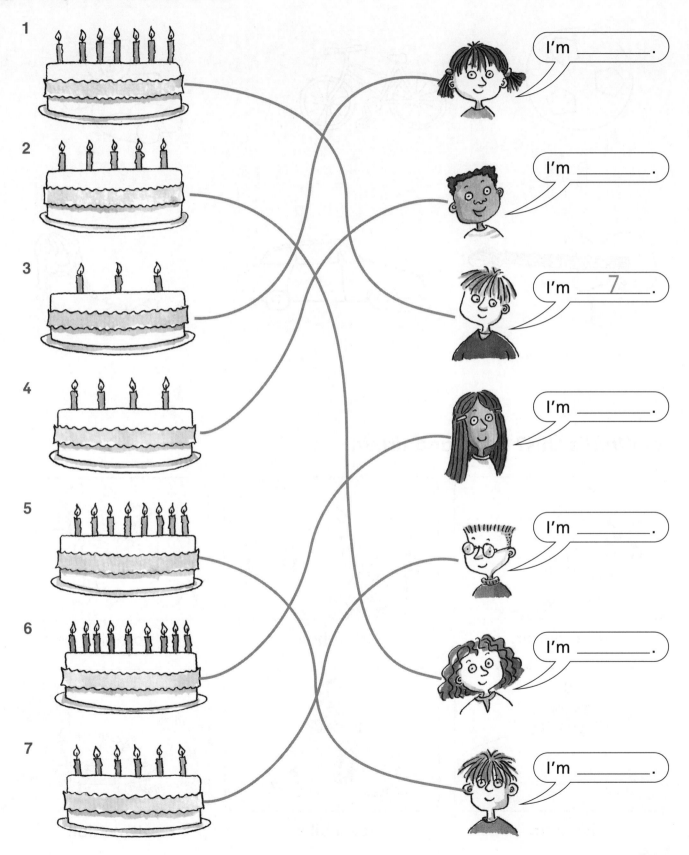

1

I'm _____.

2

I'm _____.

3

I'm ___7___.

4

I'm _____.

5

I'm _____.

6

I'm _____.

7

I'm _____.

● **Colour and write.**

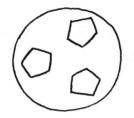

a ball   a bike   a teddy bear

a guitar   a car   a doll

● **What's this? Read and draw.**

It's a guitar.   It's a ball.   It's a teddy bear.

It's a car.   It's a bike.   It's a doll.

● ✔ **the correct pictures.**

1

2

3

4

● **Look and ✔ or ✗.**

1 Is it a guitar? ☐

2 Is it a ball? ☐

3 Is it a car? ☐

4 Is it a teddy bear? ☐

5 Is it a doll? ☐

6 Is it a bike? ☐

Colour.

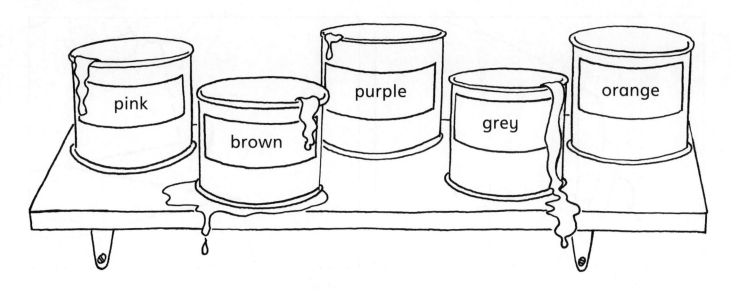

Find, circle and colour.

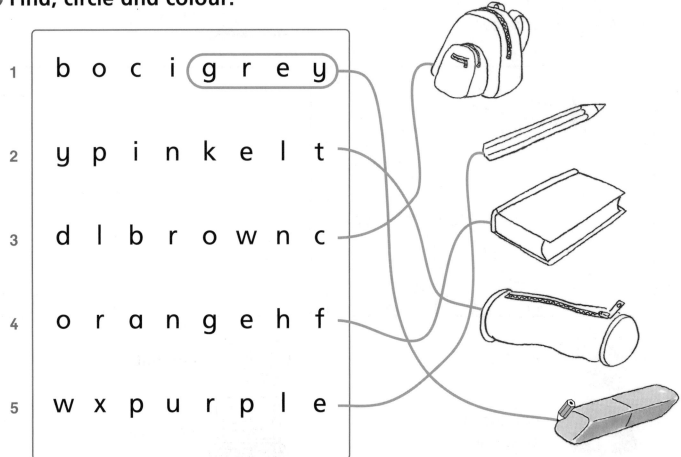

1 b o c i g r e y

2 y p i n k e l t

3 d l b r o w n c

4 o r a n g e h f

5 w x p u r p l e

LET'S GO!

● **Read and circle.**

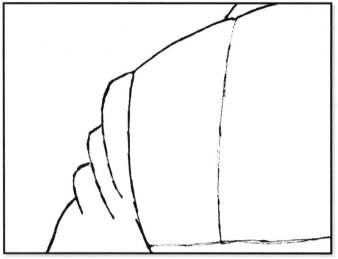

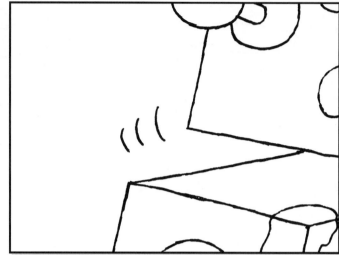

 I'm Zoko.

 I'm Zoko.

 I'm Captain Shadow.

 I'm Luke.

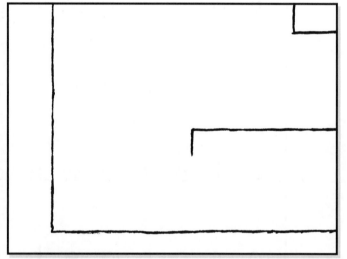

 I'm Pluto.

 I'm Pluto.

 I'm Captain Shadow.

 I'm Luke.

● Colour.

1 = brown	3 = blue	5 = purple	7 = black	9 = orange
2 = pink	4 = yellow	6 = green	8 = white	10 = red

● Answer the question.

What's this? It's a _____ .

Project time!

● **Circle the birthday pictures, then colour.**

 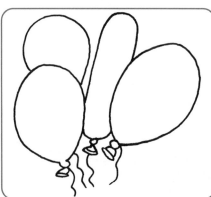 

● ✔ **and draw.**

My birthday cake ☐

My birthday card ☐

My birthday party ☐

My birthday present ☐

● **Read and ✔ the correct sentences.**

I'm hungry. ✅   I'm thirsty. ☐

I'm thirsty. ☐   I'm hungry. ☐

I'm big. ☐   I'm small. ☐

I'm big. ☐   I'm small. ☐

● **Match.**

I'm thirsty. You're hungry.   I'm big. You're small.

MISSING!

● **Number and colour.**

● **Write He's or She's.**

<u>He's</u> hungry.

_____ big.

_____ small.

_____ sad.

_____ happy.

_____ thirsty.

● **Look and complete.**

| hungry | thirsty | small | big | sad | ~~happy~~ |

1 She's …

2 He's …

3 She's …

4 He's …

5 She's …

6 He's …

1. h
   a
   p
   p
   y

2.
3.
4.
5.
6.

● **Find, circle and match.**

hamster   dog   cat

c a t f i s h h a m s t e r r a b b i t b i r d d o g

bird   fish   rabbit

● **Look and write.**

1 It's a _____ rabbit _____.

2 It's a _____.

3 It's a _____.

4 It's a _____.

5 It's a _____.

6 It's a _____.

THE LAKE CAFÉ

✔ the correct pictures.

1

2

3

4

● **Match and write.**

| cat | dog | rabbit | fish | hamster | ~~bird~~ |

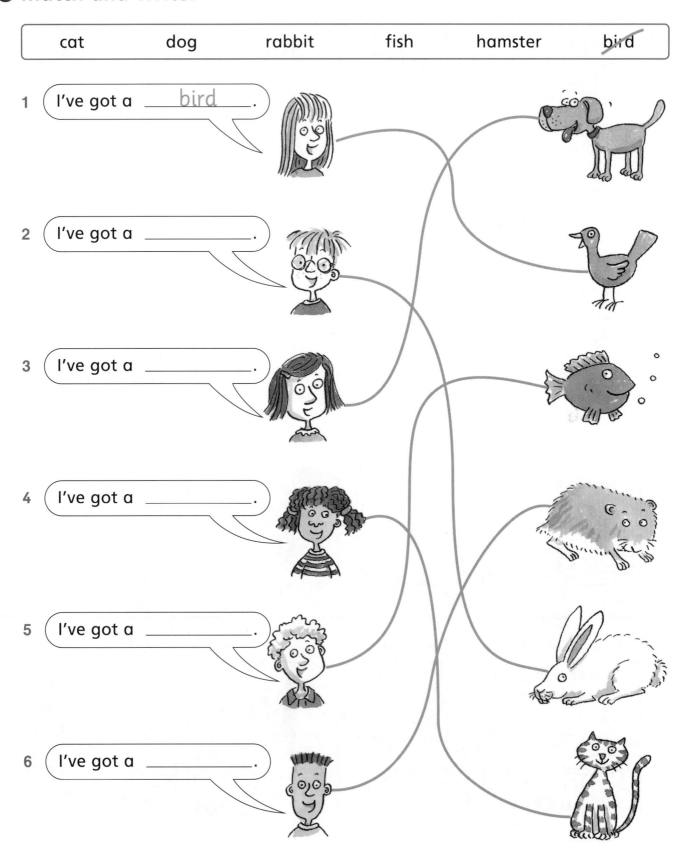

1 I've got a _____bird_____ .

2 I've got a _____ .

3 I've got a _____ .

4 I've got a _____ .

5 I've got a _____ .

6 I've got a _____ .

● **Look and number.**

an apple — 4

a donut — ☐

an ice cream — ☐

an orange — ☐

a sandwich — ☐

a sausage — ☐

● **Find, circle and write.**

1	i	t	o	(a	p	p	l	e)	e	apple
2	u	h	o	r	a	n	g	e	n	_____
3	s	a	n	d	w	i	c	h	j	_____
4	m	i	c	e	c	r	e	a	m	_____
5	y	l	s	a	u	s	a	g	e	_____
6	p	d	r	s	d	o	n	u	t	_____

THEY'VE GOT DJ!

● **Match and draw.**

Hubert

Doris

Pluto

Zoko

● **Complete the questions and circle Yes or No.**

| sausage | orange | ice cream | donut | ~~sandwich~~ | apple |

1 Have you got a _sandwich_ ?  Yes No

2 Have you got a _____ ? Yes No

3 Have you got an _____ ? Yes No

4 Have you got an _____ ? Yes No

5 Have you got a _____ ? Yes No

6 Have you got an _____ ? Yes No

● **Read and match.**

I've got an ice cream and an orange.

I've got a sandwich and an apple.

I've got a donut and an orange.

I've got a sausage and an ice cream.

● ✔, **draw and write.**

apple ☐

donut ☐

ice cream ☐

orange ☐

sandwich ☐

sausage ☐

This is my food. I've got _____ and _____ .

● **Match.**

head   hair

eyes   nose

ears   mouth

● **Look and write.**

ears	eyes	nose	head	mouth	hair

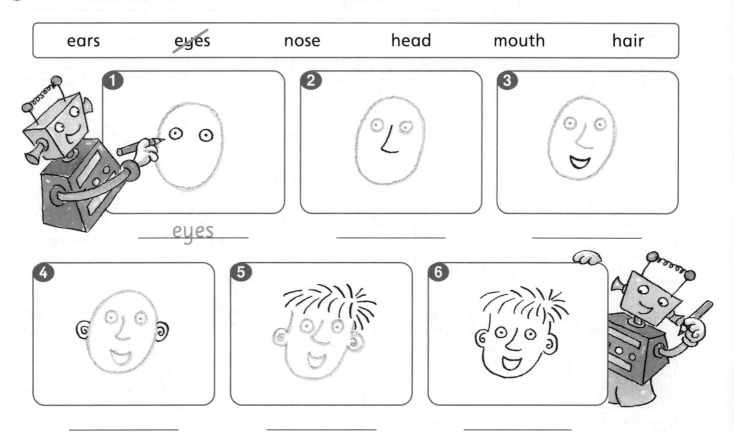

1. _eyes_

2. _____

3. _____

4. _____

5. _____

6. _____

POOR PLUTO

● **Number.**

● **Read and colour.**

1 Zeeky's got pink hair.

2 She's got blue ears.

3 She's got black eyes.

4 She's got an orange nose.

5 She's got a green mouth.

● **Complete the sentences and circle Yes or No.**

1 She's got a small ___head___ . (Yes)   No

2 He's got black _____ . Yes   No

3 She's got big _____ . Yes   No

4 He's got small _____ . Yes   No

5 She's got a small _____ . Yes   No

6 He's got a big _____ . Yes   No

● **Read and draw.**

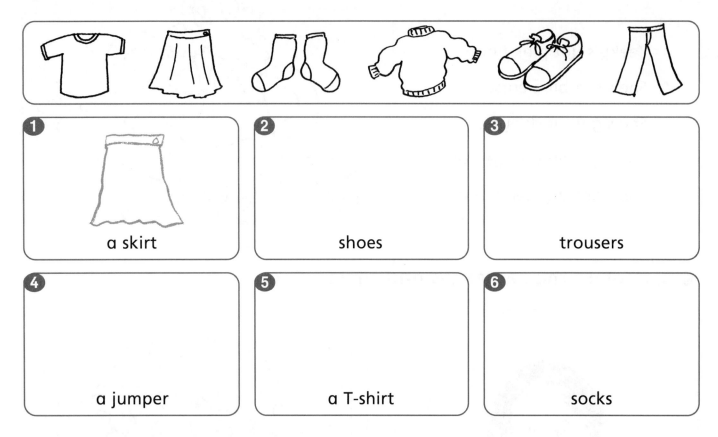

1 a skirt

2 shoes

3 trousers

4 a jumper

5 a T-shirt

6 socks

● **Complete the crossword.**

1

2

3

4

5

|6

1 | s | h | o | e | s |

2

3

4

5

● **Draw and write.**

6

It's a _____ .

DJ AND THE MOBILE

● **Colour the people and circle Yes or No.**

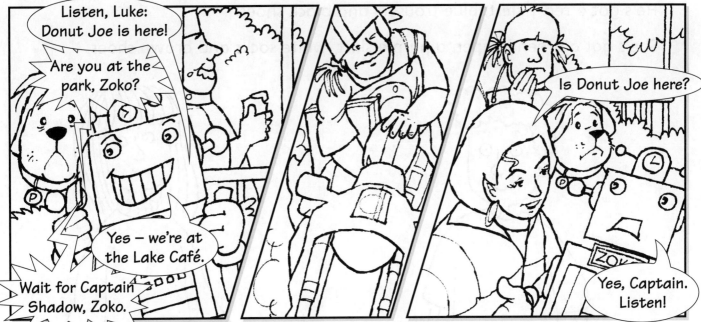

1	Chocolate Chip's got brown hair.	Yes	No
2	Captain Shadow's got red trousers.	Yes	No
3	Zoko's got green eyes.	Yes	No
4	Chocolate Chip's got a yellow T-shirt.	Yes	No
5	Pluto's got pink hair.	Yes	No

Unit 11

● **Read and colour.**

He's got a red T-shirt, blue trousers and black shoes.

She's got a green jumper, a purple skirt, white socks and brown shoes.

● **Circle He's got or She's got.**

He's got   (She's got)   a green jumper.

He's got   She's got   a red T-shirt.

He's got   She's got   blue trousers.

He's got   She's got   a purple skirt.

● **Look and number.**

a bed ⬚ 2

a box ⬚

a chair ⬚

a sofa ⬚

a table ⬚

a TV ⬚

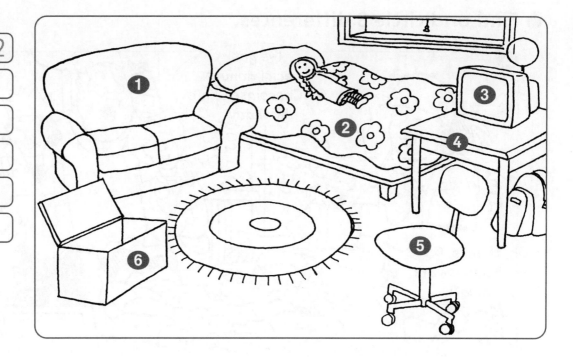

● **Look and write.**

What's this?

It's a ___TV___.

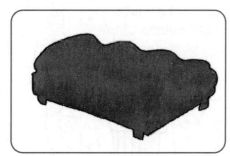

It's a _____.

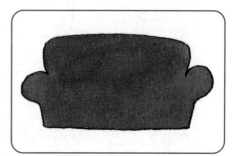

It's a _____.

It's a _____.

It's a _____.

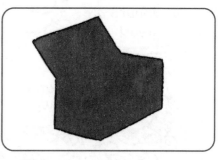

It's a _____.

HAPPY BIRTHDAY, CHOCOLATE CHIP!

● **Find and circle 8 differences.**

● **Match and write** in or on.

1	Where's the TV?	It's _____ the chair.
2	Where's the guitar?	It's _____ the sofa.
3	Where's the dog?	It's _____ the car.
4	Where's the teddy bear?	It's _____ the bag.
5	Where's the cat?	It's __on__ the table.
6	Where's the hamster?	It's _____ the TV.
7	Where's the bird?	It's _____ the box.
8	Where's the book?	It's _____ the bed.

Project time!

● **Look and** ✔ **or** ✗.

● **Complete the sentences.**

bed	✔
box	✗
chair	
sofa	
table	
TV	

bed	
box	
chair	
sofa	
table	
TV	

This is my bedroom.
I've got a ____bed____,
a _____ and a _____.

This is my bedroom.
I've got a _____,
a _____ and a _____.

● **Draw and write.**

My bedroom

This is my bedroom.
I've got a _____

_____

_____.

● **Match.**

I'm a witch. | I'm a ghost. | I'm a cat.

● **Find and count.**

● **Colour.**

1 = black	2 = white	3 = grey	4 = brown	5 = blue
6 = purple	7 = red	8 = green	9 = yellow	10 = orange

● **Draw.**

1 star

8 balls

7 presents

● **Draw some more Christmas things.**

● **Colour and ✔ the things you do at Christmas.**

● **Draw the path.**

● **Number the eggs.**

The Easter Egg Hunt

● **Colour the eggs.**

1 = red	2 = orange	3 = grey	4 = purple	5 = black
6 = green	7 = pink	8 = yellow	9 = blue	10 = brown

OXFORD
UNIVERSITY PRESS

Great Clarendon Street, Oxford OX2 6DP

Oxford University Press is a department of the University of Oxford.
It furthers the University's objective of excellence in research, scholarship,
and education by publishing worldwide in

Oxford New York

Auckland Cape Town Dar es Salaam Hong Kong Karachi
Kuala Lumpur Madrid Melbourne Mexico City Nairobi
New Delhi Shanghai Taipei Toronto

With offices in

Argentina Austria Brazil Chile Czech Republic France Greece
Guatemala Hungary Italy Japan Poland Portugal Singapore
South Korea Switzerland Thailand Turkey Ukraine Vietnam

OXFORD and OXFORD ENGLISH are registered trade marks of
Oxford University Press in the UK and in certain other countries

ISBN: 978 0 19 472820 1

Printed in China

This book is printed on paper from certified and well-managed sources.

ACKNOWLEDGEMENTS

Cover Illustration by: David Mostyn

Illustrations by: Judy Brown pp 3, 5, 6, 8, 9, 11, 12, 13, 15, 16, 18, 19, 21, 22, 23,
25, 26, 28, 29, 31, 32, 33, 35, 36, 38, 39, 41, 42, 43, 44, 45, 46, 47.
David Mostyn pp 4, 7, 10, 14, 17, 20, 24, 27, 30, 34, 37, 40.